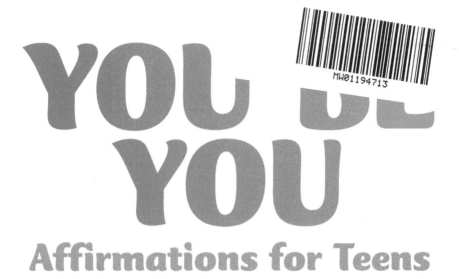

YOU BE YOU

Affirmations for Teens

Daily Motivation to Boost Self-Confidence and Feel Empowered

JOY HARTMAN, MSW, LCSW

ROCKRIDGE PRESS

Interior and Cover Designer: Scott Petrower
Art Producer: Meg Baggott
Editor: Sean Newcott
Production Editor: Jax Berman
Production Manager: Jose Olivera

Author photo courtesy of Jacek Oleszczak/Blue Sky Photography

Paperback ISBN: 978-1-63807-984-2
eBook ISBN: 978-1-63807-635-3
R0

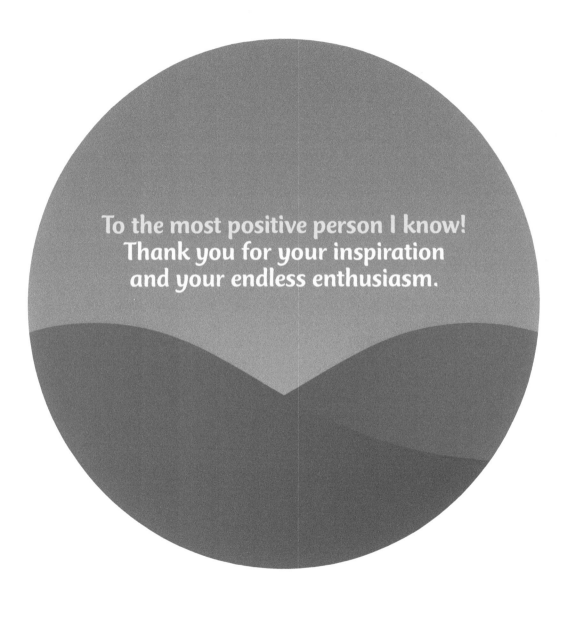

To the most positive person I know!
Thank you for your inspiration
and your endless enthusiasm.

Introduction

Welcome to *You Be You*, a book of inspiration, positivity, and affirmations.

Sometimes, life can get complicated. Drama with friends, conflict with family, school pressures, and even social media can cause you to doubt yourself and fall into negative thought patterns and difficult feelings. In such moments, the words you speak to yourself become your inner voice, creating and reinforcing your self-worth. Your words really matter. This book will show you how to speak kindly to the most important person—you!

Grab this book anytime you need a little boost or start to doubt yourself. Open it to any page, and you will find words to inspire you and get you back on track to being the unique and amazing person that you are. You'll also find stories of fellow Unstoppable Teens that are meant to inspire you. These stories range from teens honing their creativity, giving back to their community, and overcoming trauma; you might read about a teen going through something just like you, or feel motivated to embrace who you are!

Let me introduce myself: I'm Joy Hartman, a mental health therapist who has worked with teenagers and families for more than thirty years. My counseling style is called strength-based therapy, and my job has been to help people find their inner strength and use it to live the life they want and make and maintain the relationships they want to have. I'm a pro at finding the specific things that make you unique and capable, and I hope this book will make you a pro at finding your own amazing strengths.

By studying mindfulness, I've become inspired by the idea that thinking positive thoughts can lead to positive things happening. Just thinking you are amazing can lead you to feel amazing and then hopefully to behave in ways that support those thoughts and feelings. Words can be very powerful. There is great power in the word *affirm*, which means positively stating something that is true and confirmed. The wonderful thing about affirmations is that even if you don't quite believe the words yet, by stating them over and over, speaking them out loud, or writing them on a sticky note that you see every day, the words become true. It's not like waving a magic wand; rather, positive thoughts literally rewire your brain. Through affirmations, you teach your brain how to have positive thoughts in the first place. Over time, they become your default thoughts.

Think about affirmations as points on a compass or a map. You might not be at your final, empowering destination just yet, but the affirmations show you the way. If you keep following the route, you will get there. These thoughts create a positive energy in your life. Ultimately, you will be drawn to thinking and feeling differently, which leads you to acting differently and making different choices. Over time, they will become your truth.

My hope is that this book will fill you with positive thoughts, inspire you to create your own affirmations, and find your strengths and dreams along the way.

My strengths are what make me uniquely me. By finding great things in others, I am becoming a strength-finding expert. Today, I will find my own strength by seeing it in others.

When I am feeling anxious, I will remember that this feeling is just my body warning me of a perceived danger and that it is only temporary. I will take a minute to breathe and believe I will be okay.

NEGATIVE THOUGHTS AND BELIEFS HAPPEN. I WILL REPLACE EACH NEGATIVE THOUGHT WITH A LOVING AND KIND THOUGHT, ESPECIALLY IF THE NEGATIVE THOUGHT IS ABOUT MYSELF.

I will not let social media posts from my friends or even strangers take away my confidence. I know that social media does not always represent the truth.

My thoughts become my feelings, and my feelings become my actions. Today, I will think positive thoughts. I will feel joyful feelings, and I will act in positive ways.

I am rejecting the judgment of others. Their thoughts or opinions have no basis in my truth. I alone define my self-worth.

I deserve friendships that are trustworthy and mutual. I am a good friend and will meet people who can be trusted. I will not change who I am for other people.

THIS EMOTION I FEEL IS POWERFUL. BUT SO AM I, AND I CAN HANDLE THIS INTENSE EMOTION.

What is coming is better than what is gone. I may have lost a friend, but I have new friendships coming. I forgive myself.

My feelings are valid. I will allow myself to feel all my feelings. I am not an emotional mess or "too much." My feelings are just right.

Unstoppable Teen

Herat, Afghanistan, is home to an award-winning all-girls high school robotics team. The girls, known as the Afghan Dreamers, won an international competition in 2017. When COVID-19 was raging through their city and they heard their country didn't have nearly enough ventilators, they decided to find a solution. The girls successfully built a prototype ventilator using a Toyota Corolla car motor and a part from a Honda motorcycle, to give back to their community during a time of crisis and need.

"... instead of letting your hardships and failures discourage or exhaust you, let them inspire you. Let them make you even hungrier to succeed."

—Michelle Obama

I am headed in the right direction.
With time, hard work,
determination, and effort,
I will achieve my goals.

My mind is full of brilliant ideas. I will find ways to use those ideas to be successful. I will continue to dream big.

I CAN HANDLE THIS WEEK;
THE DRAMA AND THE STRESS
WILL NOT SWALLOW ME UP.

I will not allow sadness and loneliness to win. I like myself and will wait for healthy relationships to come to me.

Today, I will focus on what I can control: my thoughts, my feelings, and my actions. I will let go of what I cannot control: other people's thoughts, feelings, and actions.

It is easy for me to treat others with kindness. I am good at giving compliments and encouragement. Today, I will treat myself with the same kindness.

Mistakes happen. I will use this mistake to learn and grow and do better next time.

I AM A WORK OF ART. NOT EVERYONE SEES WHAT I SEE OR WHO I REALLY AM, BUT THE ONES WHO DO TRULY GET ME.

The words I speak have power. They can be forgiven but never forgotten. Today, I will choose my words carefully.

Today, I will do something for which my future self will thank me. I will get up and move, eat something healthy, or take care of my body in some meaningful way.

Unstoppable Teen

When Winter BreeAnne was a young teen, she felt passionate about many issues. She was frustrated that teens her age didn't know enough about civic engagement or the electoral process. So she developed a curriculum that challenged kids in middle school and high school to become more civic-minded and helped them better understand elections and voting. Her curriculum is now used in more than 20,000 schools. In 2020, she used that same momentum, spending more than 80 hours working with first-time voters to teach them how to cast their vote in the election as part of a movement she called "Vote with Winter."

"Just believe in yourself. Even if you don't, pretend that you do and, at some point, you will."

—Venus Williams

Whenever I want to quit or give up, I will remember that everything worthwhile takes effort. I won't give up. It will be worth it.

I believe in me. My ideas are valid, and I have important things to say. I deserve to be heard and valued.

FRIENDSHIPS ARE IMPORTANT. FRIENDS CAN BE POSITIVE OR NEGATIVE INFLUENCES, AND I WILL CHOOSE AS MY FRIENDS POSITIVE PEOPLE WHO ENCOURAGE ME TO BE A POSITIVE PERSON.

A little progress each day adds up to big results. Today, I will take tiny steps and trust that they are adding up to something big.

No one said this was going
to be easy. But I believe this
will be worth it soon.

Practice makes perfect. I will practice believing in myself. I will practice being kind to myself. I will practice loving myself.

Being driven by feelings of hate or competition with others only creates hatred and competition. Instead, I will strive for accomplishment and pride to create more accomplishment and pride.

FAMILY IS LIKE A BOX OF CRAYONS. EACH COLOR IS UNIQUE, BUT TOGETHER THEY MAKE A GREAT PICTURE. I WILL BE UNIQUELY ME AND APPRECIATE MY FAMILY FOR BEING UNIQUELY THEMSELVES.

Failure is not the opposite of success. It takes many failures to finally succeed. I will celebrate the failures and believe that success will come.

Staying within the lines is boring.
I am ready to be creative and
unique. The world will see something
beautiful because I ignored the lines.

Unstoppable Teen

Tragedy struck the community of Zanzibar in 2011, when a boat capsized and nearly 200 locals aboard drowned. For years, conservative Muslim cultural beliefs had dictated that women were prohibited from going in the ocean and therefore weren't taught how to swim. The Panje Project, started by a local Zanzibari woman named Khadija Sharriff, aimed to change that. Sharriff taught a group of courageous teen girls how to swim and how to prevent drownings. These teen girls acquired lifesaving skills and became the first of thousands of women and girls who have learned water safety, worn burkinis with confidence, and positively shifted their community's cultural belief about girls and the ocean.

"No matter what, people are going to like you or not like you. So be authentic, and let them like you or not for who you actually are."

—Kobe Bryant

I am allowed to cry anytime I want. My tears express my feelings, and I am proud to be a person who can express my feelings freely.

Moving on hurts and is difficult. But there is no growth if I stay stuck. Good things are coming next.

I MAY NOT ALWAYS BE EXACTLY SURE WHO I AM, BUT I AM EXACTLY SURE WHO I AM NOT, AND I WILL STAY TRUE TO MYSELF. I WILL OWN MY MISTAKES AND KEEP FINDING MY OWN WAY.

When I feel overwhelmed,
I will remember that a little
at a time gets it done:
one task, one moment, and
one thing at a time.

Today, I will practice social courage, being myself without apologizing; moral courage, doing the right thing no matter what; emotional courage, feeling all my feelings; and intellectual courage, learning something new and keeping an open mind.

I will talk to myself like I talk to my pet: "You are the cutest thing ever! I love you so much." I am also the cutest thing ever and deserving of love and attention.

Who I surround myself with makes a difference. Today, I will choose people who empower me, believe in me, support me, listen to me, and deserve me.

WHEN EMOTIONS ARE HIGH, GOOD JUDGMENT RUNS LOW. IF MY EMOTIONS ARE CAUSING SELF-DOUBT, NEGATIVE THOUGHTS, OR RECKLESS CHOICES, I WILL TAKE A MINUTE TO BREATHE. I CAN MANAGE THESE TOUGH EMOTIONS.

I know my anger triggers. I am learning my happiness triggers too. Today, I will go outside, take a walk, get coffee with a friend, laugh, or do something nice for someone.

Having gratitude for and recognizing even the smallest things can change my attitude. I will look for tiny things to be grateful for today.

Unstoppable Teen

Mo'ne Davis was only thirteen when she became the first Black girl to compete in the Little League World Series. She was also the first girl to pitch a winning game in the World Series. To top it off, she was the youngest athlete to appear on the cover of *Sports Illustrated*. Davis went on to launch her own athletic shoe line, and a percentage of the proceeds go to an organization that empowers girls around the world.

"Young girls are told you have to be the delicate princess. Hermione taught them that you can be the warrior."

—Emma Watson

Healing is recovering after a hard thing has passed. Now that my hard thing is over, I am beginning to heal.

Resilience is the ability
to thrive instead of survive,
even when life is hard.
Today, I will thrive. I will
show up and try.

COMPARING MYSELF TO OTHERS IS THE ROOT OF SHAME. WHEN I AM STRUGGLING WITH COMPARING MYSELF TO OTHERS, I WILL STAY OFF SOCIAL MEDIA.

I will talk less, listen more, watch less, move more, complain less, appreciate more, fear less, try more, compare less, and accept more.

I stand up for myself. My voice should be heard. My opinions have value. My words matter. I will speak with respect and kindness.

I am a whole, complete person and not just my body parts. I will work on loving all of me and not criticizing parts of me.

I will love myself for who
I want to be, not for what I
think others see in me.

I CHOOSE TO FILL MY MIND WITH POSITIVE THOUGHTS. I CHOOSE TO FILL MY BODY WITH HEALTHY FOODS. MY MIND AND BODY ARE STRONG AND HEALTHY.

I will let go of what I thought was supposed to happen and embrace what is happening. I will find the good in this new path my life is taking.

My mind is strong. I will fill it with powerful thoughts, which will give me positive emotions.

Unstoppable Teen

Although he was born with osteogenesis imperfecta—a rare bone disorder that causes his bones to break easily—Robby Novak is living life to its fullest. Best known as "Kid President," Novak became an inspirational motivational speaker, offering advice to adults, sharing his views on the world, and promoting kindness. He even scored an invite to the Oval Office, where he got to sit at former President Barack Obama's desk. Today, Novak continues to teach tolerance and unity to his listeners.

"Nourish what makes you feel confident, connected, contented. Opportunity will rise to meet you."

—Oprah Winfrey

I am super amazing, talented, and strong. Nothing will get in my way today.

There are so many reasons for me to be happy today.

I WON'T LET FEAR ROB
ME OF JOY. I WILL EMBRACE
THE CHALLENGE AND
TAKE THE RISK.

I should always shoot for the moon. Even if I miss, I will land among the stars.

It is okay to cry when there
is too much heaviness in life.
The clouds also rain when
they get too heavy.

Just breathe.
Sometimes that is enough.

I have doubts and insecurities.
Everyone does. Today,
I will ignore them and
focus on what I know to
be true and fair.

I LOVE MYSELF
AND APPROVE OF MYSELF
EXACTLY AS I AM.

I am on the right path.
It can be annoying and hard,
but it is still the right path
to reach my goals.

Happy people focus on what they have.
Unhappy people focus on
what they don't have. Today,
I will remember what I have.

Unstoppable Teen

After learning about conservation in school, sisters Melati and Isabel Wijsen decided to take action on their home island of Bali by reducing plastic bag use. They founded an organization called Bye Bye Plastic Bags and promoted the idea of eliminating plastic bags at school, in communities, and on beaches. Their project gained momentum. Eventually, they were able to ban all plastic bags from the airports in Bali. By 2018, their ban grew to include the entire island of Bali. In 2021, their home country, Indonesia, declared plans to cut plastic pollution completely by 2040.

"Develop enough courage
so that you can stand up
for yourself and then stand
up for somebody else."

—Maya Angelou

After every negative thought I have, I will think a positive thought.

To be truly happy, I must learn to follow my own path. I don't need anyone's approval to be me.

I WILL BE CAREFUL WHEN TALKING TO OTHERS. IT ISN'T MY INTENTION TO FAN THE FLAMES OF DRAMA.

I will remind myself to do the things I love and take time for me, even if it means I have to do it by myself.

The more I am exposed to something, the more automatic it becomes. I will surround myself with positive vibes and positive people.

Today, I will take time to love myself. The more I love myself, the less validation I need from others.

I can change my future
by changing my thoughts,
feelings, and actions today.

WHEN MY INNER CRITIC
IS MEAN, I WILL NOT
LISTEN TO IT.

I don't have to be perfect.
I just need to be me.

Anxiety means I am aware of a perceived danger. I care about my safety, and I have the power to protect myself from harm.

Unstoppable Teen

X González, Jaclyn Corin, David Hogg, and their classmates were leading normal teenage lives until the shooting of 17 students and teachers at their high school in Parkland, Florida, on Valentine's Day 2018. These survivors channeled their grief, fear, and anger into activism. They planned a rally and march in Washington, DC, that was attended by tens of thousands of people. They became the faces and voices of everyday teens who live in fear of gun violence in their schools, and they showed others that a combined voice makes a difference.

"Teens should always remember they are unique, special, and bring something to the world that no one else can."

—Tara Lipinski

I can see, hear, smell, taste, and touch my way to feeling calm.

Even if I have no idea what I am doing, I will still start.

I CAN AND WILL ASK FOR WHAT I WANT. I WILL ASK MYSELF, MY TEACHERS, MY PARENTS, AND MY FRIENDS. NO ONE WILL KNOW WHAT I NEED UNLESS I ASK.

I have the courage to love myself and shine in my own weird and beautiful way.

I won't treat people as bad as they are. Rather, I will treat them as good as I am.

I can be assertive without being aggressive. I can be a leader without being bossy. I can speak my truth, and that doesn't make me difficult—it makes me powerful.

If I worry less about everyone else and focus more on myself, then I am doing a great job.

I NOTICE THE PEOPLE WHO
ARE TRULY HAPPY FOR
MY HAPPINESS AND SAD
FOR MY SADNESS. THOSE
ARE MY PEOPLE.

When life got real, it showed me who wasn't a real friend, and that's okay.

I didn't do anything wrong. The people who benefitted from me not realizing my own strength got mad. But all I did was grow.

Unstoppable Teen

When Jack Cable was fifteen, he found a weakness in a cryptocurrency site that allowed him access to other people's accounts. He reported the bug and quickly became a leader in the cybersecurity world. He won several high-level competitions and an award from Steve Wozniak, Apple's cofounder. Jack is now in college at Stanford University, while also running a cybersecurity business that works with cryptocurrency companies to strengthen their protection against hacking.

"... if you have good thoughts they will shine out of your face like sunbeams and you will always look lovely."

—Roald Dahl

Beauty begins the minute
I decide to be myself.

I don't need to be embarrassed about my situation. Most people are struggling with something and just trying to smile through it.

I WON'T LOSE MY VOICE FOR SOMEONE WHO ISN'T EVEN LISTENING. I WILL SAVE MY IDEAS, BREATH, AND ENERGY FOR PEOPLE WHO WANT TO REALLY HEAR ME.

I will speak more kind words to myself than anyone else. I will make my internal dialogue count.

I deserve people in my life who reply quickly, who are the first to like my posts, and who want to hear my stories ten more times.

101

If I get a gut feeling about someone or something, I will trust it. My gut knows things.

I deserve friends who enjoy my particular brand of weird, not people who want me to be normal.

IT'S OKAY IF SOMEONE
DOESN'T LIKE ME.
NOT EVERYONE HAS
PERFECT TASTE.

If I choose to post on social media, I will post pictures and comments with confidence and with good intentions. It's my story. I'm just doing me.

If people can't handle me
randomly bursting into song,
they aren't my people.

Unstoppable Teen

"Ah, the fresh smell of cow poop," said no one ever! Until now. Dwi Nailul Izzah and Rintya Aprianti Miki, two high school girls from Indonesia, won first place in the countrywide science fair by creating an organic, chemical-free, inexpensively made air freshener. The process of collecting cow manure, fermenting it, mixing it with coconut water, and creating a liquid took about seven days. But the air freshener impressed the judges and is said to smell like the plants that cows eat rather than manure. Mist of cow poop, anyone?

"I encourage teens to go after what they love and not worry about their age, because the rewards of talking about things that are important to them while expanding their own knowledge are incredible!"

—Maya Van Wagenen

I don't take orders. I don't even take suggestions. I don't need to apologize because I do things my way.

Only people who are
unhappy with themselves
are mean to others.

I DON'T ALWAYS NEED TO HAVE A PLAN. SOME DAYS, I CAN RELY ON JUST COFFEE AND WEIRDNESS TO GET ME THROUGH.

Rock bottom has a basement, so I'd better start climbing these stairs. When I think I'm at my lowest, I'll keep climbing.

I won't let my mind bully my body. If I've thought or said anything unkind to my body, I will apologize and be grateful for what I have.

When life gives me a hundred reasons to cry, I will find a hundred reasons to smile.

I'll never let anyone treat me like regular glue.
I am glitter glue, and I will keep sparkling.

I'M TOO BUSY GROWING
UP AND MAKING A LIFE
TO WORRY ABOUT SOMEONE
ELSE'S DRAMA. THEIR DRAMA
ISN'T MY PROBLEM.

How I speak about others says a lot about me. I will identify and appreciate the strengths in others, even when I am annoyed with them.

If I could believe in the tooth fairy
for years, surely I can believe
in myself for a minute.

Unstoppable Teen

Keep an eye on Keagan Roberts, one of the youngest, openly gay elected officials in the United States. Keagan wanted change in his hometown of South Berwick, Maine. He missed the deadline for his name to appear on the ballot for town council, but he got his name out by standing outside the town hall all day on election day to make sure people voted for him as a write-in candidate. It worked! He got elected in 2019 at the age of nineteen. Keagan is showing the world that every vote matters, and that teens can make a difference.

"It takes courage to grow up and become who you really are."

—e.e. cummings

Not every path is paved.
I will be brave and go off-road
to find my adventure.

Sometimes it's best to just walk away. There is no need to say mean things, fight it out, or find common ground. When it's done, it's done.

BREAKING SOMEONE'S TRUST IS LIKE CRUMPLING UP A PIECE OF PAPER. IT CAN BE SMOOTHED OVER, BUT IT'S NEVER THE SAME AGAIN. I PROMISE TO TAKE CARE OF THE RELATIONSHIPS THAT MATTER TO ME.

I am just beginning to grow.
No one starts out an expert.
But watch me go.

I am strong enough to be alone, but brave enough to know when I need help and courageous enough to ask for it.

I walk forward with purpose and my head held high. I'm not afraid to look life right in the eyes and hold the stare.

I am a masterpiece and
a work in progress all at once.
Today, I will work hard to
make me great.

I WILL NOT LIE AWAKE AND WORRY ABOUT WHAT OTHER PEOPLE THINK OF ME, BECAUSE I AM STILL GOING TO BE ME.

If I work out, it's because I love my body and celebrate its strength and abilities, not because I see room for improvement.

I feel confident in my body. I can find small details that I love about how I look, feel, and move. My body is beautiful and unique, and I will take good care of it today.

I have all that I need to be a great friend. I am trustworthy, kind, and a great listener. I am ready to meet someone who is all those things for me too!

Forgiving someone who hurt me shows I am strong and confident. I will work on accepting their words of remorse as truthful.

IF I HURT SOMEONE'S FEELINGS, I WILL TAKE ACCOUNTABILITY AND WORK ON FORGIVING MYSELF.

I am not perfect and will make mistakes sometimes, but I will be a better person because I am working on growing and learning from my mistakes.

No one can define who I am or who
I am not. I am uniquely me, and only
I get to define what that means!

I have a lot to offer the world, even if I am not quite sure what that is yet. I will find my voice and learn to use it my way.

Just because my path is different from other kids' doesn't mean I'm lost. It means I'm an adventurous person who likes to pave my own way.

Resources

Books

A Year of Positive Thinking for Teens: Daily Motivation to Beat Stress, Inspire Happiness, and Achieve Your Goals by Katie Hurley, LCSW

The Mindfulness Journal for Teens: Prompts and Practices to Help You Stay Cool, Calm, and Present by Jennie Marie Battistin, MA, LMFT

Apps

Grateful: A Gratitude Journal
This app focuses on helping users embrace gratitude, which has been shown to lead to positive thinking and experiences.

I am—Daily Affirmations
This app aims to help users transform negative thoughts into positive, helpful ones. It claims to improve confidence and raise self-esteem through positive affirmations.

Happify
Based on the principles of positive psychology, this app is designed to help you create research-based habits to help you live a life filled with happiness.

Louise Hay Affirmation Meditations

These daily affirmation meditations are meant to help users think positively. Your thoughts influence your feelings. In turn, those thoughts and feelings can influence the choices you make.

ThinkUp

This app mixes daily affirmations with your choice of music and pictures. You can even use your own voice to read the affirmations.

Websites

Crisis Text Line

This is a resource for any teen struggling with mental health. Text HOME to 741741 to get support 24/7. CrisisTextLine.org

Happify

Find out your happiness score so you can start improving it today with activities designed to achieve greater life satisfaction. Happify.com

TeensHealth

This site covers all things related to teen health, including physical, emotional, and mental health. KidsHealth.org/teen

Teen Ink

This website and national teen magazine showcase teen creativity through writing, art, and photography. TeenInk.com

TreePeople

This movement was started by a teenager more than 40 years ago. Teens can join the movement and get involved in many different conservation and environmental causes. TreePeople.org

References

Awad, Monique. "Afghanistan's Girls' Robotic Team Breaks New Paths." UNICEF. December 24, 2020. UNICEF.org/afghanistan/stories/afghanistans-girls -robotic-team-breaks-new-paths.

Bill & Melinda Gates Discovery Center. "Winter BreeAnne Mobilizing Voters." 2021. DiscoverGates.org/exhibition/wethefuture/young-leaders/winter-breeanne.

CBC Kids. "5 Inventions Changing the World!" 2021. CBC.ca/kidscbc2/the-feed /5-inventions-changing-the-world.

CBSNews.com. "The Inspiring Life of the 'Kid President.'" March 4, 2013. CBSNews.com/pictures/the-inspiring-life-of-the-kid-president.

Elder, Jeff. "Meet the 20-Year-Old Super-Hacker Who Was the Youngest Member of the Pentagon's 'SWAT Team of Nerds' and Is Now Fighting for Election Security with Homeland Security." *Business Insider*, October 20, 2020. BusinessInsider .com/election-hacking-jack-cable-hackerone-dhs-cisa-vote-2020-10.

Green School Bali. "Melati & Isabel Wijsen." 2021. www.GreenSchool.org/bali/alumni -stories/melati-isabel-wijsen.

Munnik, Jo. "Inside 'Burkini Island' Where Muslim Girls Learn to Swim." CNN. February 1, 2019. CNN.com/travel/article/zanzibar-style-swimming-intl/index.html.

Olito, Frank. "11 Inspiring Stories of LGBTQ Teenagers that Have Moved the Internet." *Insider*. June 15, 2020. Insider.com/inspiring-stories-of-lgbtq-high-school -teens-2020-6.

Svrluga, Barry. "Seven Summers Later, Baseball Remains Mo'ne Davis's Calling." *The Washington Post*. June 9, 2021. WashingtonPost.com/sports/2021/06/09/mone -davis-broadcaster-dc-grays.

Time Staff. "TIME's 25 Most Influential Teens of 2018." *TIME*. December 10, 2018. Time.com/5463721/most-influential-teens-2018.

Acknowledgments

Thank you to the many teens I've met through the years. Your strength and belief in yourselves and in one another are an inspiration. Teens are some of the most passionate, positive people I know.

Thank you also to Callisto Media for this opportunity to share affirmations and positivity in this book for teens. I am grateful for your guidance and support as I navigated the world of publishing.

About the Author

 Joy Hartman, MSW, LCSW, is a licensed clinical social worker based in Wisconsin. She is passionate about empowering teens to become strong, confident adults. She believes every teen has unique strengths, and she uses those to help them build resiliency. As the parent of three teenagers of her own, Joy's experiences guide her in supporting teens and parents as they navigate challenges and mental health concerns. Follow Joy on her blog at JoyHartman.com or on Facebook at Facebook.com/JoyHartmanLCSW.

CPSIA information can be obtained
at www.ICGtesting.com
Printed in the USA
JSHW011224261221
21522JS00001B/1